Maximize Your Mind; Peak Your Potential!

100+ Ways to Boost Your Brain & Achieve Your Goals

Marlene Caroselli
Robin Wilson

Published by the Center for Professional Development
324 Latona Road, Suite 1600
Rochester, New York 14626

The authors are available for conferences, keynotes, and training
programs. Robin Wilson is an associate with the Center and
founder of Reach and Achieve Associates, a professional coaching,
training, and mentoring firm. Her coaching programs have been
the catalyst for change for leaders and entrepreneurs since its
inception in 1997. Training programs include coaching for leaders,
managing change, listening, communications, and creating
behavioral change. Visit her web site (www.reachandachieve.com)
or e-mail her at Robin@ReachandAchieve.com. You may also
contact her at 585-218-9350.

Dr. Marlene Caroselli founded the Center for Professional
Development in 1984 and since that time has trained thousands of
working adults in leadership, management, creativity, problem-
solving, quality, and communications programs--both nationally
and internationally. A prolific author, she is a frequent contributor
to Stephen Covey's *Excellence* publications, the *Customer Service
Journal*, and a host of other magazines and newsletters. Visit her
web site--http://hometown.aol.com/mccpd--or contact her at 585-
227-6512 or mccpd@aol.com.

ISBN 0-922411-11-5

From the American Heart Association comes advice for combating stress:

Assert yourself.
Eat and drink sensibly.
Stop smoking.
Exercise regularly.
Relax.
Be responsible for what you can control.
Let go of what you can't control.
Reduce the causes of stress.
Ask for help.
Set priorities.
Pace yourself.
Take time for yourself.
Examine your values and live by them.
Set realistic goals.
Sell yourself to yourself.
Remind yourself of what you do well.

These recommendations apply to fitness on several levels--physical, mental, emotional. We'll concentrate especially on the mental in order to make the following words of wisdom more than black lines on white paper, in order to maximize your mind and to peak your potential.

"I merely took the energy it takes to pout and wrote some blues."   --Duke Ellington

"Cease to gnaw that crust! There's ripe fruit above your head."   --Henry David Thoreau

We'll examine, in general, the aspects of your job, and possibly your life, that you wish you could exert more control over. We'll consider the fact that for any given situation, you can leave it as it is, make it worse, or make it better. There are no other choices.

Ideally, you'll opt to make those less-than-ideal circumstances better than they are. If so, your pro-active choice will be dependent, in very large measure, on the development of self-confidence. And, there's a causal connection between self-confidence and improved cognitive processes.

Can you create and fulfill your own prophecy? Can you honestly become more brain-powerful? Can you really optimize your cognitive capacity? Can you truly maximize your mental operations? Yes, Yes, Yes, and Yes. But...not if you're always telling yourself you're slow, you have a poor memory, you can't do math, et cetera. The first step then in Mind-Maxing is to think both positively and powerfully.

EX LIBRIS

Books make the best furniture.

Memory:

The Seven Sins of Memory by Daniel Schacter lists
Transience (weakening of memory over time), Absent-
mindedness, and Blocking as Sins of Omission; and
Misattribution, Suggestibility, Bias (unconscious editing of
previous experience), and Persistence (recall we'd rather
forget) as Sins of Commission. Consider how one or more
of these sins (of omission or commission) could cause
trouble for you.

The best memory tip in the world is to make associations
(the wilder, the better) between the thing you want to
remember and some known entity.

Other tips include a mnemonic device (rhyme, alliteration,
a visual image, repetition, a schema or system).

Of course, practice never hurts:

3	87	901	5201	84215	075328	40152856
		104867624		6903457182		

5	26	738	9320	52916	380157	6281302
		392815647		2753019586		

Other than names, what is it you most need to/want to
remember better? Figure out a device for greater recall.

Problem-Solving:

Critical thinking, according to learning theorist Jerome Bruner, involves the ability to "go beyond what is given." In a similar vein, the top competence identified by the federal government for those aspiring to executive service is "external awareness." And, GE's former CEO, Jack Welch, notes, "When the rate of change outside the organization is greater than the rate of change inside the organization, then we are looking at the beginning of the end." Make a prediction, note a trend, or issue a warning for the future, based on the events of the present.

Caution: If you view every problem as a nail, you will always hit it with a hammer. Vary your methods: the problems you face are varied enough to require different approaches. For example, can you think of three ways to solve the problem that follows?

There are eight employees at a meeting. Each one shakes hands just once with each of the others. What is the total number of handshakes?

Keep in mind what H. L. Mencken said: "For every complex problem, there is one solution that is simple, neat, elegant.....and wrong!"

Synesthesia, and its psychological cousin, autonomy -of-object, explore concepts from different perspectives. They'll widen your appreciation of diversity and of Peter Drucker's view of violins.

Good problem-solvers persevere--they don't perseverate.
The following combination of letters, representing a
sentence from which one particular vowel has been
removed, illustrates what we mean. Figure out what letter is
missing, insert it in nine different places, and you'll be able
to figure out what the sentence is saying.

VRYFINXMP
LARXCDSWH
ATWXPCT

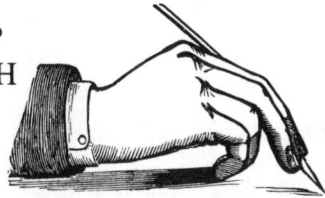

Asked how he came upon the polio vaccine, Jonas Salk
replied, "I learned to think like Mother Nature." Looking at
problems from different perspectives often affords insights
we might not have had otherwise. State a work-related
problem and then consider it from the eyes of a politician,
an environmentalist, a priest, a police officer, an
entrepreneur, a scientist, a musician, et cetera.

Tom Peters once remarked, "If you have gone a
whole week without being disobedient, you're doing
your organization and yourself a disservice." To foster
the symbolic disobedience of which he speaks, try
this. List ten specific things (policies, procedures,
philosophies, practices, processes, paperwork,
meetings) that you have been doing for a long time.
Then explore a rebel's option.

7

deal: lead
time: emit
letter
parent

Listening:

"The essence of genius," according to William James, "is to know what to overlook." And, author Mitchell Posner urges us to be "ecologists" as far as information is concerned. In the center of a clean sheet of paper, draw a circle. Then extract three key words, from a verbally-inflated set of instructions, and write those words in the circle.

Work with a friend. Ask him or her to talk about an enjoyable experience and to stop unexpectedly. You are to take one word from the last sentence uttered and use it to begin speaking about something *you* enjoy doing. Stop unexpectedly and have the other person continue the conversation using one word from the last sentence you spoke.

Both the major prophets and minor prophets were painted in Michelangelo's Sistine Chapel. Cherubim are shown at the ears of both. However, only the major prophets appear to be listening. According to John Curtis Brown in *The Journal of Creative Behavior*, this distinction explains the difference between genius and talent. Comment on his assertion.

List 20 barriers that can impede the listening process. Then determine which you can control. Finally, engage in a dialog that refutes Dr. Leo Buscagli: "Most conversations are just alternating monologues—the question is, is there any real listening going on?"

Consider these questions:
1) Why do we listen?
2) What do people listen for?
3) Who would you like/do you like to listen to?
4) What are the barriers to effective listening?
5) What part do nonverbals play in the listening process?
6) Share a time when you felt you were really listened to.
7) Why do you think it's said that some people talk too much but it's never said that some people listen too much? Explain.
8) How do you account for these figures from the University of North Alabama: 75% of what we hear, we hear wrong and of the remaining 25%, we forget 75% within weeks?
9) What, if anything, do you do when you feel you're not being listened to? If you do nothing, why is that your choice?
10) What is the cost of poor listening—personally and professionally?
11) What words/phrases are emotionally-charged as far as you're concerned?

Creativity:

Creativity is the result, in very large measure, of the belief that we are creative. To develop your creativity muscles, periodically ask yourself: "What if...?" and "What use...? questions.

Convergent responses are typical, expected, logical. For example, asked how one gets to Heaven, you'd probably say something like "Follow the Golden Rule." Ask this question of a divergently-oriented child, though, and you might hear, "Go to Hell and take a left!" Think divergently about these questions:

What letter is clearly, visibly, obviously out of place?

b | c
---
d | g

What number does not belong with the others?
   3810   6024   4816   1452

What letter belongs in the blank?
   OTTFFSSE _____

What letter belongs in the blank?
   DJ FM AM JJ AS O _____

Think of the symbolism associated with causes and colors. For example, we tied yellow ribbons on trees to show support for hostages in Iran. If the head of your organization asked you to create a new ribbon design, what would it look like? What message would it express? What initials would be meaningful? What color would capture your organization's mission?

One of the best ways to engender creative possibilities is to put things together that normally are not aligned. (Anne Geddes did this with babies and vegetables.) List ten disparate items: "peacock" and "eraser," for example. Then search among those items for a solution to a workplace problem or for an improvement to an existing situation.

Einstein regarded imagination as more important than knowledge. (He imagined chasing sunbeams in space.) Imagine unusual scenes to describe your workplace.

Concentration:

You can train yourself to focus on input with practice like this. Listen intently to information you want to/need to retain. Do not permit environmental distractions to block input. (Earl Woods did this with Tiger.) Assess how well you actually concentrated.

To prevent your mental energies from being dissipated, you must sometimes give yourself a pep-talk before undertaking a challenge. What would that talk sound like? Once you've devised it, apply it to this challenge.

This is Tic Tac Toe in reverse. For you to win, the other person must *lose* by having three X's in a row. Here's the game so far. What move can you make now so that your opponent loses with three X's in a row?

```
    |   |
 X  | X | O
 ___|___|___
 O  |   |
 ___|___|___
    | X |
    |   |
```

Try this: Think of six six-letter words—"muscle" and "carpet," for example. Take three pairs of them and print them like this, as neatly as possible.

[m c] [u a] [s r] [c p] [l e] [e t]

12

When you're concentrating intently, you're unaware of time. Interestingly enough, time seems to be both suspended and rushing by. Make time work for you by being the first among competitors to figure this out: What is the first number (start with zero and continue with whole numbers in ascending order) that, when spelled out, has all the letters of that word in alphabetical order?

Research from psychologist Ralph Erber at the University of Virginia found that concentration on a challenging task lessens depression, relieves stress, and gets your cerebral juices flowing. Visualization helps as well. What visions do you use prior to beginning a difficult task?

Describe the conditions that surround you when you are "in the zone" or having a "white moment." (These are the times when your concentration is at its most intense.)

Learning To Learn:

Zipf's Law of Least Effort states that we're more inclined to express ideas (internally and externally) that require little effort than ideas that are complex or confusing. (Think of Tuckman's assessment of teaming: Form, Storm, Norm, Perform.) Write a full page about something you know well. Then reduce it to a Zipfean concept.

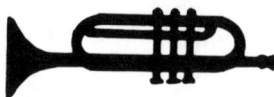

Aristotle asserted that "man is the most imitative of living creatures, and through imitation learns his earliest lessons." What do you now know that you've acquired through "observational learning"? Then, think about those you'd describe as "super-learners." What can you learn from them about the learning process?

The retention rate from lectures, according to the National Training Laboratories of Alexandria, Virginia, is a mere 5%. By contrast, if you use the knowledge immediately and/or teach it to others, you can raise the retention rate to 90%. Take some new knowledge and either apply it immediately or teach it to a colleague.

"Tomorrow's illiterate," Herbert Gerjuoy asserts, "will not be the man who cannot read; he will be the man who has not learned how to learn." When acquiring information for the first time, set up "advance organizers."

Reasoning:

Professor John Goodlad of the University of Washington maintains that students in U.S. schools use less than one percent of their school day in exchanges that call for reasoning. Try "Then-izing" to project possible future consequences. Consider the possibilities. Explore ramifications of actions. Anticipate likely scenarios and objections.

Sometimes you have to go beyond the obvious, beyond the surface, beyond your own perspective in order to consider the multiple shades of gray in which black/white issues are usually embedded. Consider these questions.

What do these words have in common:
        red, pink, gray, brown, black?
Which city is least like the others:
        Seattle, Wichita, Dallas, Atlanta?
Which letter does not belong:
        N Y F M H K Z?
Which pair completes the analogy:
        note: Eton:: school:dean or paper:pupil
        or message:school or time:emit?

Janusian thinking asks you to look at things from opposing points of view, to question the givens, to propose the novel. The creators of Columbo did this when they decided to reveal the "perp" in the opening moments, instead of at the end, where we usually learn "whodunit." Take a situation you're facing (as an employee, resident, family member or friend), eliminate the assumptions that surround it, and look for a unique, viable way to handle it.

Early learning makes the unfamiliar familiar and later learning makes the familiar unfamiliar. Explain this statement in the clearest possible terms. Then take ten additional statements that contain paradoxes or complexity or chaos. Reason through them and then write a paraphrase of what you think the thought's originator meant.

The first stage of learning is confusion.

Organization:

Patterns of organization—of which there are dozens—expedite expression by offering a framework within which ideas can be logically and cohesively conveyed. Here are some of the most popular:

Chronological FDP/FLP Inductive Deductive
Order of Importance Problem-Solution Topical.

Learn to stratify. Draw five or six boxes and then, in response to a given prompt, begin filling them in, not necessarily in a linear fashion.

One efficient way to gather your thoughts and express them admirably —even if you've not been given much preparation time—is to use the Pro 'n' Con'D Method. It requires you to explore the pro's or advantages inherent in a given situation; then, to examine the disadvantages or con's; and finally, to consider what elements of the proposal need to be developed/debated/ discussed/defined further.

Whether you're asked to respond orally or in writing without much preparation time, you can organize your thoughts quickly using the O-F-T method. (It'll make you sound as if your brain's on steroids.) State your opinion. Support it with facts. Summarize by using the word "therefore" in your final sentence.

Quick-wittedness:

According to Lee Iacocca, the best thing you can do for your career is learn to think on your feet. The more you practice, the quicker and more lucid you will become in your expression. An excellent practice technique is to have a friend ask you a series of challenging questions over an extended period of time.

Try this: Use the PPF structure to present a seamless response: cite the Past, mention the Present, allude to the Future.

Carry on a conversation using only questions.

Use the KWIC method of replying to an unexpected question: State the Kernel of your remarks. Widen its basic thrust. Illustrate your point. Conclude.

Challenge yourself. Take two absolutely unrelated words and create an intelligent link between them. If you'd like to be Herculean in your attempt, take *three* unrelated words and form a logical connection among them. Go beyond the obvious into the realm of the awe-inspiring.

Develop verbal fluidity by writing as fast as you can in response to an external prompt.

Originality:

You'll be remembered for your words as well as your actions. And since, in a given day, you employ more words than you undertake actions, you have a greater chance of being remembered (positively we hope) for what you've said. Avoid the obvious ("Most fires are caused by some igniting source coming into contact with combustible material") and the erroneous (The only thing I know about Philadelphia is that it's in New Jersey") and the illogical ("Let's have some new cliches"). Examine memorable words others have expressed to understand the power of memorability.

Thousands of years ago, Aristotle noted that to understand the metaphor is the beginning of genius. Consider famous metaphors (Iron Curtain, Glass Ceiling, Rainbow Coalition) and then create several of your own: to describe the relationship between employees and managers, to depict a national problem, to define your brain at work.

Think of the inspirational three- or four-word phrases that have long motivated others. "Never give up" from Winston Churchill, "Just do it" from Nike, "Don't look back" from LeRoy Satchel Paige. Think of five short exhortations designed to improve a situation at work.

Chiasmus is the term for a two-part sentence: the second half uses some of the words expressed in the first half but uses them in such a way that a whole new meaning is created. An example would be this observation from Plato: "Wise men talk because they have something to say; fools, because they have to say something." Try creating a chiasmus of your own, something profound enough to deem you an original thinker.

Japanese firms doing business in America often use the bathtub exercise as part of their hiring process. Apply it to a workplace problem your group regards as critical in nature.

Make lists: things you love, things you hate, things that could be improved, things people complain about, things that annoy you, things that you see every day, things that always work as they should, et cetera.

Then select two things from any of the lists. Combine them. Experiment, explore, envision. Seek an innovation. Keep doing this until you have one viable possibility.

Read in a field that has nothing to do with what you do for a living. Keep a notebook of interesting ideas from your reading. Then apply something you've learned to a situation you face at work.

Seeing the Big Picture:

On his deathbed, Hubert Humphrey spoke of his "irreducible essence"—the core, fundamental belief that governs microcosmic and macrocosmic, individual and organizational behavior. What principles govern /should govern your life /your work?

Futurists Naisbitt and Aburdene encourage us to think about the information we receive daily and what it is really telling us. Step back and try to see the big picture in the following items.

1. What's the pattern in this arrangement?
   86, 11, 4, 90, 1, 7, 16, 12, 28
2. What's the holiday?
   ABCDEFGHIJKMNOPQRSTUVWXYZ
3. What the root cause of current workplace issues?

Try to see a scenario that is larger than the literal as you read the following. A man gets out of prison and pushes his car to a hotel, where he leaves quite a bit of money. Then, he pushes the car to a nearby house, where he again leaves money but not as much. Explain what's happening.

Definitions help clarify the direction in which we're moving/should move/should not move. Describe a current workplace issue. Then, before you begin finding resolutions, clearly define the issue.

21

Verbal Fluidity:

Verbal fluidity is the ability to express yourself smoothly without fumbling or mumbling or stumbling as you do so. (It's great if you have a high IQ, but that's no more than a lottery ticket. *Winning* involves putting that IQ to work. It's not enough to *be* smart; you have to *sound* smart, too.) Practice by making as many five-word sentences as you can, using these letters as the first letters in each of the five words:

A-B-C-D-E.

A Scottish proverb notes that those who wish to be leaders must also be bridges. We admire those who can bridge two thoughts, who can transition between what's being said and what needs to be said. Bring a conversation smoothly around to a point you'd like to make.

A study by Martin and Powers found that stories carried greater credibility-power than statistics. Having a few true examples that illustrate broad points will help develop the fluidity factor. If possible, use stories based on events you've personally experienced.

On a regular basis, have a colleague ask you a challenging question (or toss out an interesting quotation) and respond to it with no preparation time at all.

22

Persuasion:

According to Ken Blanchard, the key to leadership today is influence, not authority. Whom do you want or need to influence? To do what? What things does that individual value? What general persuasion techniques have you found effective?

Peter Drucker, father of modern management science, maintains that leaders know how to ask questions, the right questions. What particular questions will assist you in shaping and delivering your message?

Describe a situation in which you wish you'd been more persuasive. Outline a new influence-message and incorporate two of these five techniques: Cite precedent, Cite statistics, Go out on a verbal limb, Liberate competence, and Look at the big picture.

Vision has been defined by Jonathan Swift as the art of seeing the invisible. Describe a work-related vision powerfully enough to invite others to support your cause.

Deliver a persuasive message based on one or more of these alliterative techniques:

Anecdote
      Advance preparation
         Advantages
            Achievement
               Audience
                  Assurance
                     Analogy
Advocate
      Authority
         Analysis
            Antecedent
               Anticipation
                  Aphorism
                     Agreement
Appeal
      Arousal
         Arch
            Adventure
            Allure
               Assay

Drama
      Deprecation
         Decency
            Developments

Evidence
      Experience
         Excitement
         Exploration

Fulfill Your Own Prophecy:

Feed your brain, which contains billions of cells called neurons. Daily, we lose thousands of these cells--depending on the toxins we're exposed to--pesticides, stress, alcohol, and preservatives among others. While the brain uses a fifth of our energy supply, it only weighs three pounds. Ongoing research confirms that what we eat has a direct impact on how we think.

Studies by Dr. Marilyn Albert of Harvard confirm these factors as critical for a well-functioning brain: education, activity, and the psychological well-being that comes from knowing what you do makes a difference.

Dr. Jay Lombard and Carl Germano, among hundreds of other experts, recommend lowering your intake of fats, sugars, and caffeine; and eating organic, deep-colored fruits and vegetables, and fish and fowl rather than red meat.

Drs. Abram Hoffer and Morton Walker recommend B, C, and E vitamins; zinc, calcium, and magnesium, fatty acids, and DHEA.

Develop your genius-genes. Incorporate these methods:

1. Think in opposite terms; make unusual or unrelated connections and combinations. Develop your senses.
2. Conceptualize in as many different forms as possible.
3. Apply metaphors.
4. Read outside your field.
5. Question.
6. Observe and note interesting occurrences. Keep notebooks and logs. Pride yourself on your curiosity.
7. Challenge the existing order. Remain confident.
8. Keep your brain active.
9. Achieve a "concert" state in which ideas can "flow."
10. Tolerate ambiguity.

11. Explore.
12. Maintain a child-like approach to new ideas.
13. Learn from others.
14. Be "disobedient."
15. See the invisible.
16. View problems as opportunities.
17. Think divergently.
18. Escape mental restraints.
19. Develop mental and verbal fluidity.
20. Better your personal best.

Take calculated, not foolhardy, risks. Be encouraged by Jack Welch, former CEO of GE and the "Manager of the Century," who defines success as reaching out and grabbing all life has to offer. And by author Anais Nin, who acknowledges that sometimes it's more painful to remain "tight inside the bud" than it is to blossom.

If you have a vision and are actively working toward it, you can be said to be fulfilling your own self-defined prophecy. Ideally, with daily dosages of "vitaminds," you can achieve *all* you envision. More (brain) power to you!

Integrity:

"Courage is not limited to the battlefield or the Indianapolis 500 or bravely catching a thief in your house. The real tests of courage are much quieter. They are the inner tests, like remaining faithful when nobody's looking, like enduring pain when the room is empty, like standing alone when you're misunderstood."   --Charles Swindoll

An important leadership trait is personal integrity. Webster defines integrity as a "rigid adherence to a code of behavior." Integrity is evident when actions reflect your values and beliefs; when you live up to your word; when there is consistency between what you believe, what you say, and how you act.

People with integrity know what they want and their actions reflect that knowledge. Integrity involves living and learning on a daily basis, integrating what you do in your career with what you do in your personal life. How many times are you late for an appointment and don't call to let the person know? How about saying you'll meet a deadline and then missing it without advising the other person that you need an extension? How about lying or stretching the truth? Dishonesty shows a lack of integrity and hinders the development of trust.

When trust or integrity is lacking, performance is hampered. To perform at your peak requires behaving in a way that generates trust and closeness with others.

Here are some tips and questions to help you develop personal integrity:

1. Know yourself. What are your strengths and weaknesses? If you don't have a clear picture of yourself, then it's difficult to adhere to ethical standards.

   Make a list of your strengths and weaknesses. Be as objective as you can. Then ask someone else you know and trust to do the same for you. Compare the two lists.

2. Become the kind of person you wish to be. Life-long learning and personal development are essential to integrity.

   Read every day, at least one book a month. There is no substitute for reading in order to expand your personal/professional boundaries.

3. Make a list of the things you do that others may regard negatively. Remember, being abrasive or taking another's credit or violating a company policy reflect a lack of respect. And, respect lies at the heart of integrity. Take action on the areas that you have identified as being potentially negative.

Take this simple test. If you act this way over 50% of the time, check Yes; if less than 50%, check No.

1. I have a defined set of values and my actions reflect those values. Yes_____ No_____

2. I follow through on my commitments to others.
   Yes_____ No_____

3. If I am going to be over ten minutes late for an appointment, I call to let the person know.
   Yes_____ No_____

4. I follow through on my promises.
   Yes_____No_____

5. I am open to other points of view and willing to try new things.   Yes_____No_____

6. I strive to understand others before making quick judgments.   Yes_____No_____

7. I develop lasting relationships with people around me.   Yes_____No_____

8. My words and actions demonstrate support for the people around me. Yes_____ No_____

9. I deal fairly with other people when problems or issues arise.   Yes_____ No_____

10. I encourage others to succeed and don't feel threatened by their success.
    Yes_____No_____

11. I am trusted.   Yes_____No_____

Consider these ethics-related questions.

1. What situations or events cause me to act in a less than ethical manner?
2. In what situations or events do I usually demonstrate a high level of integrity?
3. Who are the people with whom I need to spend more time?
4. Who are the people with whom I need to clear up misunderstandings?
5. What are my values?
6. What things do I feel passionately about?
7. What are my goals? Do these goals support my values and beliefs?

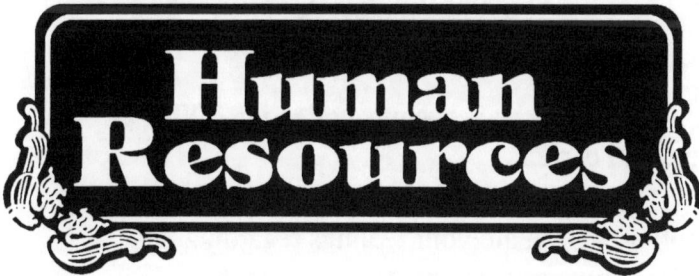

Human Resources

Decision-Making:

When making a decision, try using the **CREATE** model.

C = Creating the vision of what you want the outcome of the decision to be.

R = Reflecting back on earlier decisions that you have made. What did you learn that could help you make this decision?

E = Empathizing with other people who are affected by this decision. Try putting yourself in their shoes.

A = Acting. Any decision without a plan of action and follow-through is doomed from the outset.

T = Thinking about the best course of action. What are some potential barriers?

E = Emoting. What are your feelings regarding this decision? Get the facts and balance them with your intuition.

Think about a decision you need to make and use the above formula to formulate a plan. Then act on it right away.

Ayn Rand states, "In order to live... act; in order to act make choices."

What decision have you made that you are not taking action on? What choices do you need to make in order to act? Why have you not taken action on that decision?

Sometimes, when making a decision, it is important to think creatively. To help with that, try this exercise:

Remove six letters to find the common word that remains.

Sibxrolcectotelrsi

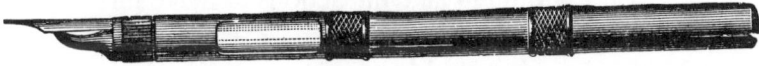

In The *Professional Decision Thinker*, author Ben Heirs maintains that an increasing number of social, political, commercial, environmental, and legal consequences are associated with decisions of considerable import. Select an important decision you have to make. Then make five (or more) columns. At the top of each, write a possible consequence associated with this decision or an area that might be impacted as a result of implementing the decision. Proceed to explore some of the consequences that might result from implementing the decision.

What decisions do you need to make in order for opportunities to become reality?

Consider these questions the next time you have to make a decision:

1. What's the best outcome that can occur?
2. What's the worst thing that can happen?
3. Who will be affected by this decision?
4. What are the action steps that need to be taken after the decision is made?
5. Do we have the resources to implement the actions?
6. What is the timetable for the decision? What is the timetable for the follow-up action steps that will need to be taken?
7. Is the timetable realistic?
8. Am I willing to take the actions to make this decision a reality?
9. Am I ready and able to continue moving forward?
10. Am I willing to accept responsibility for the outcome of this decision?

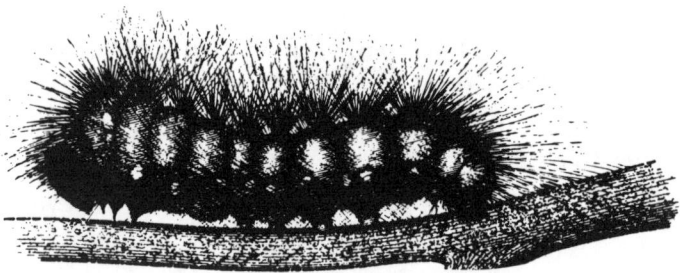

Remember this the next time you need to make a decision.

VISION + PASSION + ACTION = SUCCESS

Vision – Having a clear vision gives you the direction you need for those moments of decision. Vision can act as a compass and a homing device to guide you to your destination. Guy Hendricks and Kate Ludeman in their book *The Corporate Mystic* note, "Most business failures are failures of vision. By contrast, a clear vision often is the first step on the road to success."

What is the vision that can guide you toward making effective decisions?

Passion – Being passionate gives you the confidence and the power to take a risk. Such depth of feeling gives you the determination to do what is necessary to achieve what you want.

What issues/situations are you most passionate about?

Action – There is no substitute for action in achieving your goals. If you don't move, you will never get where you want to go. What decisions can you act on today?

Success – It is difficult to measure the effectiveness of decisions without defining what success would look like. What does success mean to you? How would you know if you had achieved it?

Interpersonal Skills:

Communication is one of the most important skills you can have today. How would you rate your communication skills?

Ralph Nichols from the University of Minnesota conducted research on how we spend our time communicating. These were his results:

40% Listening
35% Talking
16% Reading
9% Writing.

How do you spend the majority of your communicating time? Do you listen more than you speak or speak more than you listen?

Don Peterson, former Ford CEO says, "Results depend on relationships." Think about the results you are expected to achieve in your position. Who are the key people that can help you achieve those results?

Now think how you would rate your interpersonal exchanges with the key people that you identified. Use a scale of (low) one to ten (high). If you rated some of exchanges low, what specific steps can you take to improve the relationships? If you rated them high, what specific elements will add to that successful relationship?

Unclear communication causes confusion and conflict. To illustrate, take a look at this communication:

A woman was overheard saying, "That person's mother was my mother's mother in law." What relative is she talking about?

Studies show that much of our communication is non-verbal: we communicate through our body language and with our words. Body language often reveals the emotions that we may be trying to hide. When you communicate, be aware of your body language. Does it match your words?

The words we use can have a profound impact on our communication; one word can change the entire meaning of an expression. Take a look at these statements. What changes could be made to improve their effectiveness?

"If you had done what I had asked, none of this would have happened."

"I don't agree with you…"

"I understand that but…"

"Your report has been late the last two months. Why can't you get it to me on time?"

"How did you let that happen?"

You can respond positively or negatively to someone's communication. Take a look at these statements and reword them to show a more appropriate response.

"Been there. Done that."

"I'm not the only one who makes mistakes."

"It's not my fault. I just did what I was told."

In our interpersonal communications, we can either bring people in or shut them out. An example of bringing in might be asking someone for his or her thoughts. Shutting-out can appear in the form of interruptions.

Make a list of five statements that bring a person into a conversation and then make a list of five statements that shut others out.

Conflict Resolution:

Conflict can directly affect productivity. Yet, disagreements are often not brought out in the open for fear of repercussions. List three appropriate ways to openly bring up conflict.

Conflict can often be handled in a non-confrontational manner--by asking questions and understanding the other person's point of view while stating your own. Think of additional ways to address conflict that are non-confrontational.

It is common for people to rush in with a quick response without fully understanding the situation. Questions help us understand and show the other person we are listening.

Below are some questions to aid in understanding and clarifying.

> "What were your thoughts on that?"
> "I don't understand. Can you explain it to me?"
> "What were the reasons for your decision?"
> "What are the options or possibilities?"
> "When did you want the information for your
>   report?"

Your perception of people can affect the way that you respond to them. If you see people as being very competent and having good ideas, you are more likely to listen and try to understand. However, if you perceive people as being incapable, you will rush in to judge, criticize or find fault. Think of people that you work with. What is your perception of them and how does that affect your interpersonal exchanges?

Fear impacts our communication. If we are insecure in our abilities or feel threatened in some way, we tend to react more than respond. Think of a recent event in which you felt fearful or threatened. How did that feeling influence your communication? What are your options the next time you feel that fear or insecurity?

Time Management:

"Where does all my time go?"

"It seems I can never get done everything that needs to be done."

"My to-do list keeps getting larger."

Do these statements sound familiar? In this day and age, a lot is expected of people in their personal and professional lives. If you are to be truly successful in your life, time management is essential!

The first stage of time management is determining how you spend your time. For the next two weeks, keep a time log of all your activities. Include everything on the list, even social breaks. After two weeks, review your logs. Where was most of your time spent? Did any patterns emerge? What percentage of your week's time did you have control over? What percentage did you not have control over? Was your time spent in the way you thought it was being spent? How much time was spent doing the "urgent" tasks that took time away from your important tasks? As a result of this analysis, what changes will you make in how you spend your time?

One key factor in managing your time is to know what is important to you. Once you know what the "Big Rocks" (primary values and key goals) are in your life, it is easier to prioritize your life around them.

Make two lists of the things that you value most. Make one list for your personal and another for your professional life. Narrow that list down to ten and then to three in both areas. Then determine three key personal and three professional goals for the year. Once you have your top three, prioritize your daily activities around them. Determine which kept you from achieving those top priorities.

A time-waster is an activity that keeps you from doing the "important" task and achieving an objective in the best way possible. Some examples of time-wasters are:

> Procrastination
> Telephone interruptions
> Cluttered work area
> Lost or misplaced items
> Lack of deadlines
> Meetings
> Non-scheduled visitors
> Excessive socializing.

Now make a list of your own. Try to include ten time-wasters on your list. Choose one time-waster and commit to taking action on it now.

When you want to prioritize your activities, try this: Make a list of the top three things that you want to accomplish today that relate to the goals and values you established earlier. Then draw a line and list all your other priorities for the day. Accomplish everything above the line before starting any activity below it.

Alec Mackenzie, time management consultant, reports that the "stacked desk" syndrome (a desk with its top covered with all kinds of papers) affects more than 90% of all managers. To assist with this and other time-related problems, try these suggestions.

1. Have a place for everything and keep everything in its place.
2. Generate as little paperwork as possible.
3. Delegate everything possible.
4. Throw unneeded items away.
5. Ask questions to minimize confusion and avoid reinventing the wheel.
6. Plan what you're going to say on a phone call before making it.
7. Write things down in a notebook during the day as you think of them. Avoid using scratch paper.
8. If you're a deadline person, give yourself deadlines for completing key projects. Hold yourself accountable to that deadline or have someone else hold you accountable.
9. Learn when and how to say "no."
10. Plan. Spend time daily to plan your days, months and years. Remember to align your plans with your goals and values.

Make the three "Ps" of Time Management part of your daily routine:

Practice: Every day, practice time management. Plan and prioritize your day.

Persistence: Keep working on managing your time, even if it seems futile to do so. Time management is a process and you will see the results "in time."

Patience: Be patient and kind to yourself along the way. Don't expect perfection.

Vow to make time management a habit. (Doing something for at least 21 consecutive days can make it a habit.)

Balance personal time with work time. Try these tips.
1. Take time for rest and relaxation.
2. Let some things go. Don't worry about what has to be done or hasn't been done.
3. Exercise and work off tensions.
4. Accept what can't be changed.
5. Get away from a difficult situation or tough task; take some time to gain a new perspective.
6. Take care of yourself, physically, emotionally and mentally.
7. Surround yourself with positive, supportive people.
8. Maintain a positive attitude.

Remember: it's your time. Make choices that support your goals and move you forward.

Leadership:

True leadership is much more than a position. It is a way of life. Take a look at the word "l-e-a-d-e-r" below.

L = Live. Live and lead by example. Be a positive role model for others in all that you do in your career and at home. Leadership encompasses all roles and areas of life. It requires self-development, knowing your strengths and weaknesses and learning by the experiences that life offers you. Leading by example means taking responsibility for your mistakes and not being afraid to admit them.

E= Empathize. Understand others and value their contributions. So often we are quick to judge others without really seeing or appreciating what is being said or done. Empathy involves putting yourself in their shoes and seeing things through their eyes. Stephen Covey says, "Seek first to understand and then to be understood." In this society, we tend to want to rush in and "fix" things with our advice or knowledge. Yet, we can only fix *after* we truly understand the situation.

A = Act in a positive manner. Negative emotions can prevent leaders from realizing their full potential. Optimistic leaders with their can-do attitudes make obstacles appear surmountable and barriers seem removable. Colin Powell says that optimism is a force-multiplier. When you display a positive attitude and reflect it in your daily actions, you'll inspire others to act in a similar fashion. Thus, the force of enthusiasm helps expedite the work to be done.

D = Decide. Make important decisions while valuing the input of others. People tend to vacillate between making decisions very quickly without gathering important information, and taking more time than necessary. This vacillation causes delays. Try to align time with the value of the decision to be made.

E = Empower. Empower others to do their best by showing confidence in their abilities and giving positive feedback. Many of us are quick to judge and find fault with others. We are more likely to see the negative and respond to that, than to "accentuate the positive." Take the time to compliment and value others daily. Praise builds confidence and inspires positive action. Empowerment recognizes and develops the efforts of others.

R = Relate. Concentrate on building strong relationships, ones that withstand the test of time. Building these relationships means spending time with important people in your life. Avoid putting tasks firsts and relationships second. Reverse that trend. Put people first and tasks second. Jim Rohn says, "One of the greatest gifts you can give someone is the gift of attention."

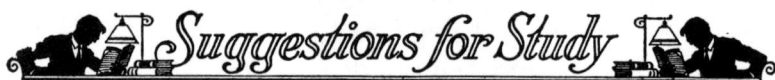

Suggestions for Study

In which one of the areas above are you strong? Which ones would you like to develop more? Take time to assess your strengths and weaknesses and start practicing your leadership skills in everyday life. When you practice these skills, you become stronger in every area.

Think about these questions as you examine your own leadership abilities.

1. On a scale of (low) one to ten (high), how much do you influence those around you?
2. As a leader, is more of your time spent giving answers or asking questions?
3. How clear is your vision?
4. What is your passion? How does it fit into organizational goals?
5. Do you act in a manner consistent with the organization's values and mission?

Complete this simple assessment to gauge your leadership abilities. On a scale of (low) one to ten (high), rate your skills in the following:

1. Introduce needed change, even if it is unpopular.
2. Lead meetings in a productive and timely manner.
3. Motivate others to meet and exceed their goals.
4. Communicate ideas in a clear and concise manner.
5. Make sound decisions in a timely manner.
6. Invest time in improving skills and abilities.
7. Resolve issues that are affecting productivity and effectiveness.
8. Involve people in decisions that affect their work.
9. Give people the information and training they need to effectively do their jobs.
10. Praise people regularly.

Take a simple inventory of your strengths and weaknesses. Have someone else that you know and trust complete a similar list for you. What opportunities lie ahead for you as a leader? What are the potential obstacles that could hamper those opportunities?

John F. Kennedy observed, "Leadership and learning are indispensable to each other." Keep a knowledge-and-awareness journal. Strive to learn one new thing each day and write down what you've gained.

Leaders have traits that make them successful, such as honesty, creativity, and courage. Think of some famous leaders and specify ten traits they possess. Which ones do you posses?

Think of leaders that you do not admire. What traits and behaviors do they display?

A successful leader is able to motivate others. List positive ways you can motivate those you lead. What are potential negative motivators?

Benjamin Disraeli once remarked, "The secret of success in life is to be ready for an opportunity when it comes." Think of five ways to prepare for future opportunities.

Understanding & Managing Change:

In today's economy; change is constant. Organizations must change and change again to stay vibrant. Employees must adjust to the changes that will be thrust upon them.

William Bridges, in his book *Managing Transitions, Making the Most of Change,* describes transition (the reorientation process that happens inside of us as a result of change) in three phases. These phases are endings, the neutral zone (time of uncertainty and chaos), and new beginnings.

Understanding and managing change and transition are critical to success for both the organization and its employees.

Think about a change your organization is going through and contemplate these questions.

1. What are the benefits to the change?
2. What challenges does this change bring to the organization and to the people?
3. What do you need to do to adjust to the change?
4. How long will it take for this change to occur?
5. What is ending for people as a result of this change?
6. How do you expect yourself and others to respond to this change?
7. What emotions is the change stirring in you and others?
8. How are these emotions being dealt with?

Kurt Lewin's change model--Thaw, Change, Re-freeze--requires managers to spend considerable time preparing others for the change they have probably had thrust upon them (as opposed to a change they've selected for themselves). The process of converting resistance to receptivity, of defrosting or melting down the old to make room for the new, begins with understanding.

Understanding--the thawed state--is achieved through discussion of comments such as these. Karl von Clauswitz, Prussian military strategist: "Beware the brilliance of transient events." Napoleon Hill: "Every adversity carries with it the seed of an equivalent or greater benefit." Author Wess Roberts: "Destiny is as destiny does. If you believe you have no control, you have no control." J. C. Penney: "I am grateful for all my problems. After each one was overcome, I became stronger and more able to meet those that were still to come. I grew in all my difficulties."

Additional considerations on which discussion should be focused include:
> What lies behind the change?
> Is there any way you can make it "not happen"?
> Given its seeming inevitability, what can you do about the change?
> Of your choices, which is the most beneficial?
> What possible benefits might evolve from the change?
> Is the rate of change likely to increase, decrease, or remain the same in the future?
> How have we as a nation demonstrated an ability to change?

What role does technology have in facilitating or
   impeding change?

If more information was produced between 1965
   and 1995 than was produced between 3000
   BC and 1965, what information-adaptations
   do we need to make as a society?

What can you do to lead the change rather than try
   to stop it?

What mistakes do people/organizations make when
   it comes to change?

What are possible linkages between stress and
   change?

What new priorities have emerged/will emerge with
   the (proposed) change?

What changes do you need to make in order to
   accommodate the internal changes?

What aspects of the change can you control?

What can't you control?

If you were leading the change in your organization,
   how would you do so?

Why do you think people cling so desperately to the
   past, to the familiar, to the known?

The second step in this change model involves introducing
the actual change. This step depends on good speaking and
writing skills. Among the elements that constitute good
communications are:

√   Providing a comfortable forum in which concerns can be aired

√   Anticipating objections and having convincing responses ready

√   Citing benefits

√   Including and addressing all the people and things that will be impacted by the change

√   Demonstrating empathy

√   Offering hope for the future

√   Repeating the message in both a repetitive and non-repetitive fashion.

The third step, making the change an organizational reality, requires superb planning: what sequence of steps, under what conditions, involving which people, will facilitate changing to the new reality? To quote Danny Ozark, Philadelphia Phillies manager: "Half this game is 90% mental." Supervising change successfully is often a question of changing mental attitudes. And such changes take both time and careful planning.

Supervisors who serve as a substantial bridge between the old and the new during the time of change make change easier to accept. You can bridge the chasm of chaos by taking the old and familiar and placing them in new and exciting circumstances.

Self-Confidence:

"You cannot go any higher than your self-image."
                              --John Maxwell

An important ingredient in your recipe for career success is having a healthy self-image. When you feel good about yourself, people feel good about you. A person who has self-confidence and inner knowledge takes greater risks because he or she is not afraid to take action, is not worried about failure. A person with low self-confidence can feel more isolated and may have difficulty relating to others. These individuals are very capable of high achievement; yet they often fail to meet their goals.

Take a look at this assessment and rate yourself on a scale of one to five for each item. Know that self-confidence is not an either/or situation, such as "I have self-confidence" or "I have none." Rather, it is a quality that varies according to circumstances.

Statements Reflecting   Statements Reflecting
High Self-Confidence   Low Self-Confidence

(very true) 5   4   3   2   1 (not at all true)

Achievement and Accomplishment

_____I am usually happy.

_____I expect to succeed in performing important tasks.

_____I feel as important as most people.

_____I would not change many things about myself.

_____I have high self-confidence.

_____It is easy to express my feelings.

_____I feel as successful as most people.

_____It is easy to meet new people.

_____I often take the initiative.

_____I feel as intelligent as most people.

Statements Reflecting   Statements Reflecting
High Self-Confidence   Low Self-Confidence
(very true) 5   4   3   2   1 (not at all true)

Valuing Myself and Others

_____I have several friends.

_____I often spend free time in the company of others.

_____Most people I know like me.

_____I am not easily depressed.

_____I am as nice looking as most.

_____I am usually relaxed and at ease with myself.

_____My feelings are not easily hurt.

_____I rarely feel uneasy without knowing why.

_____I am not often upset.

_____I do not worry a lot.

_____I feel comfortable receiving compliments.

_____I enjoy complimenting others on their
      accomplishments.

Statements Reflecting High Self-Confidence	Statements Reflecting Low Self-Confidence

(very true) 5   4   3   2   1 (not at all true)

Acting on What I Believe

_____People generally like my ideas.

_____Most people respect my views.

_____I find it easy to express my views and opinions.

_____I know what values are important to me and
      I act on them.

_____ I am comfortable expressing an unpopular opinion.

Franklin Delano Roosevelt said, "The only limit of our realization of tomorrow will be our doubts of today." What self-doubts are holding you back? Make a list of them and take action on at least one.

Think about these questions as you take a look at your own level of self-confidence.

1. What are the major achievements in your life?
2. How often do you share them with others?
3. In what ways do you value your time, money, and relationships?
4. In what ways don't you value them?
5. How much time do you spend building or nurturing your key relationships?

Make a list of all of your accomplishments. Don't judge them as being too trivial to write down. Pick the ten that you are most proud of and share them with someone you know.

Wayne Dyers once said, "It's none of my business what other people think of me." How often do other people's opinions bog you down?

What do you feel passionate about? Are you taking action on that passion?

Here are some ways to develop your self-confidence:

Make a list of what you would like to accomplish for the future. Prioritize and take at least one action on the first one. Continue taking action on your important goals until they are all met. Then set new ones.

Acknowledge your most important relationships and nurture them daily, weekly and monthly.

Monitor your self-talk.   If it's negative, reframe it.

Take care of your immediate environment. What kind of image does it portray of you? How does it make you feel?

Coaching:

Effective performance is important at every level of an organization. Coaching is designed to increase individuals' potential as well as their performance. The role of the coach is to trust in the coachee's natural abilities while providing opportunities for learning and development through questions, support, structure, and feedback.

Consider these tips when working on performance-related issues.

Ask questions rather than tell. Let the coachee do most of the talking.

Use "why" questions sparingly. They can put a person on the defensive.

Have the coachee set the goals. The coach's job is to clarify, support and set up accountability factors.

Support the coachee in designing an effective action plan that is detailed, realistic and has timetables.

Help the coachee determine potential barriers to achieving the goal.

Help the coachee see and create options and opportunities.

Use these questions to guide your coachee through the process:

1. What are you going to do?
2. What options or opportunities are available to you right now?
3. On a scale of (low) one to ten (high), how confident are you about achieving this goal? What would it take to make the confidence-level a ten?
4. What would create the kind of results you are looking for?
5. Who can support you?
6. How much control do you have over this outcome?
7. What resources will you need? Where can you get them?

The coach's role is to assist the coachee in gaining awareness of some of his or her negative behaviors. One way to do this is to have the individual think about a habit he or she would like to change. Next, encourage him or her to develop a more positive behavior and to make it a habit.

For example, if being chronically late is a habit the coachee would like to change, he or she would attempt to be on time for all commitments for a whole month.

Remember, coaching is a process and not a quick fix. The goal for coaching is behavioral change and change does not happen overnight. Peaking performance--your own or another's--takes time. But...it is time profitably spent. The returns on your investment of time will yield great rewards --both personal and professional.

Recommended Reading:

The 21 Irrefutable Laws of Leadership by John Maxwell
The Brain Wellness Plan by Dr. Jay Lombard and Carl
      Germano
Building Trust at the Speed of Change by Edward Marshall
Coaching for Performance by John Whitmore
Co-Active Coaching by Laura Whitworth House
The Effective Executive by Peter Drucker
Flow: The Psychology of Optimal Experience by Mihaly
      Csikszentmihalyi
Good to Great by Jim Collins
The Inner Game of Work by Tim Galloway
The Journal of Creative Behavior by John Curtis Brown
Leaders: Strategies for Taking Charge by Warren Bennis
      and Burt Nanus
The Leadership Challenge by James Kouzes and Barry
      Posner
Leadership Is an Art by Max DePree
Managing Transitions by William Bridges
The Oz Principle by Roger Connors et al.
The Portable Coach by Thomas Leonard
The Professional Decision Thinker by Ben Heirs
The Seven Sins of Memory by Daniel Schacter
Smart Nutrients by Drs. Abram Hoffer and Morton Walker
Thinkertoys by Michael Michalko
The Thirty-Second Sell by Milo Frank
The Time Trap by Alec Mackenzie
What a Great Idea! by Chic Thomson

ARE YOU LATERALIZED?

COLUMN 1   COLUMN 2

1. Sit in a relaxed position as you are reading this. Fold your hands in your lap. Now look at your hands. Which thumb is on top?   *left   right*

2. Assuming you could only have the foot patrol or a helicopter to locate a lost child in a park, which would you prefer?   *patrol   'copter*

3. If you were to learn a new dance, is it easier for you to read about the steps or to watch as others do the dance?
                    read   watch

4. Are you an organized person?   *yes   no*

5. Do you pride yourself on being prompt? *yes   no*

6. When you purchase a new appliance, do you prefer to try to make it work on your own or are you inclined to read the instruction manual?   *try   read*

7. Do you prefer the status quo or do you welcome change?   *status quo   change*

8. When you are driving and pull over to ask directions, do you write down what the person tells you or simply try to "see" the route in your head?   *write   see*

9. In a class, do you take copious notes or listen and digest the information?   *notes   listen*

10. Do you like to collect "stuff"?   *yes   no*

WHAT'S YOUR NATURAL BENT?

<u>Directions</u>:   First, do NOT show this page to the person being tested. You will read ten questions to that person. The answers are unimportant. What IS important is the direction in which the person is looking as he or she answers the questions. If he or she looks to the left, write "L" in the blank space. If he or she looks to the right, write "R" in the space. If he or she looks straight ahead, write "S" in the space. Make certain that the direction is *the other person's left or right*, and not your left or right. Read again.

Then, give your partner these instructions: "I'm going to give you a series of problems to solve. You cannot use paper or pencil to solve them. Take a reasonable period of time to solve them, but solve them 'in your head.' Once you have an answer, tell it to me. If you wish, I can repeat the question, once."

1.   How much is 42 x 12?   _____
2.   How many states have names that begin with a vowel?   _____
3.   Name the heads of four nations.   _____
4.   Add 2048 and 59.   _____
5.   Name five high-school friends.   _____
6.   Is 482763 the same as 367284 read backwards?   _____
7.   Count backwards by 7 from 100.   _____
8.   If the word MAT is written below WAS and WON is written below MAT, will the word SAW be written on the diagonal?   _____
9.   How many letters are there between M and V in the alphabet?   _____
10.   Is the product of 3 x 3 x 2 x 2 half or less than half the product of 9 x 8?   _____

IS YOUR MIND'S AGE YOUR BODY'S AGE?

Experiment 1

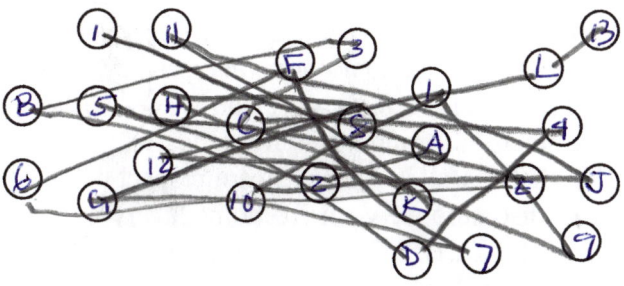

Experiment 2

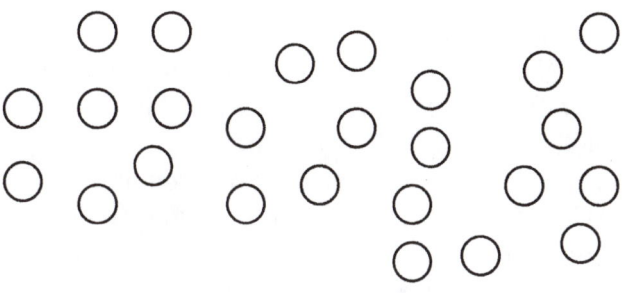

20-29; 122 / 30-39; 114 / 40-49; 145 / 50-59; 148 /
60+; 228

Based on research by Edward Coffey at the Henry Ford Health
Sciences Center in Detroit, Michigan.

63

ANALOGIES

1. NUMEROUS: POLYGON:: circumference:circle or hypotenuse:triangle or point:line or four:square

2. LOG:VOYAGE:: plan:action or minutes:meeting or route:trip or itinerary:tour or transcript:court

3. EXPURGATE:PASSAGES: defoliate:leaves or cancel:checks or incorporate:ideas or invade:privacy

4. PHARMACIST:DRUGS:: psychiatrist:ideas or mentor:drill or mechanic:troubles or chef:foods

5. CONQUER:SUBJUGATE:: esteem:respect or slander:vilify or discern:observe or freedom:slavery

6. ENGRAVING:CHISEL:: printing:paper or photography:camera or etching:acid or printing:ink

7. HUNGER:RAVENOUS:: economy:miser or sleep:drowsy or desire:activity or pain:excrutiating

8. TAUNTS:TEMPER:: gasoline:fire or ideas:revolution or words: music or catalyst:chemical

9. DECIBEL:SOUND:: calorie:weight or volt: electricity or area:distance or color:light

10. MEN:ANTHROPOLOGY:: events:history or life: zoology or children:pediatrician or clients:lawyer

11. HOMONYM:SOUND:: synonym:same or antonym:meaning or acronym:ideas or psyeudonym:fake

12. ABACUS:CALCULATING: typewriter:printing or pearls:decorating or telescope:seeing or car:speed

13. WAR:BOOTY:: sports:trophy or marriage:divorce or poor:charity or victim:spoils or politics: graft

14. CATAPULT:MISSILE:: bow:arrow or ancient:modern or arsenal:munitions or quiver:shaft

15: MARKSMANSHIP:HUNTER:: bull's eye:target or precision:surgeon or medal:soldier or bait:fisherman